Divine Poems
Göttliche Gedichte

MOTSCHI VON RICHTHOFEN

Paperback: 978-1-969919-45-9
eBook: 978-1-969919-46-6
Library of Congress Control Number: 2025922897

This is a work of fiction.

Ordering Information:

Prime Seven Media
518 Landmann St.
Tomah City, WI 54660

Printed in the United States of America

Danke an das alte und neue Testament, an Buddha's Schriften, und an die KI, die gute Recherche macht, einige gute Ideen hatte und bei der Dichtkunst noch einiges lernen darf.

Thanks to the Old and New Testaments, to Buddha's writings, and to the AI, which does good research, has some good ideas, and still has a lot to learn about poetry.

„Die größte Wohltat, die man einem Menschen erweisen kann, besteht darin, dass man ihn vom Irrtum zur Wahrheit führt."

„Welches Geschenk auch immer wir jemandem geben, das erste Geschenk, das wir ihm geben, ist, ihn zu lieben."

"The greatest benefit you can do for a person is to lead them from error to truth."

"Whatever gift we give to someone, the first gift we give them is to love them."

Thomas von Aquin

Freundlichkeit in Worten schafft Vertrauen.
Freundlichkeit im Denken schafft Tiefe.
Freundlichkeit im Geben schafft Liebe.

Alle Dinge haben Zeiten des Vorangehens und Zeiten des Folgens,
Zeiten des Flammens und Zeiten des Erkaltens,
Zeiten der Kraft und Zeiten der Schwäche,
Zeiten des Gewinnens und Zeiten des Verlierens.

Deshalb meidet der Weise Übertreibungen, Maßlosigkeit und Überheblichkeit.

Kindness in words creates trust.
Kindness in thought creates depth.
Kindness in giving creates love.

All things have times of going before and times of following,
times of burning and times of cooling,
times of strength and times of weakness,
times of winning and times of losing.

Therefore, the wise man avoids excess, excess, and arrogance.

Lao Tse

Grenzen der Menschheit (Wolfgang von Goethe)

Wenn der uralte,
Heilige Vater
Mit gelassener Hand
Aus rollenden Wolken
Segnende Blitze
Über die Erde sä't,
Küß' ich den letzten
Saum seines Kleides,
Kindliche Schauer
Treu in der Brust.

Denn mit Göttern
Soll sich nicht messen
Irgend ein Mensch.
Hebt er sich aufwärts,
Und berührt
Mit dem Scheitel die Sterne,
Nirgends haften dann
Die unsichern Sohlen,
Und mit ihm spielen
Wolken und Winde.

Steht er mit festen,
Markigen Knochen
Auf der wohlgegründeten,
Dauernden Erde;
Reicht er nicht auf,
Nur mit der Eiche
Oder der Rebe
Sich zu vergleichen.

Was unterscheidet
Götter von Menschen?
Daß viele Wellen
Vor jenen wandeln,
Ein ewiger Strom:
Uns hebt die Welle,
Verschlingt die Welle,
Und wir versinken.

Ein kleiner Ring
Begränzt unser Leben,
Und viele Geschlechter
Reihen sich dauernd
An ihres Daseyns
Unendliche Kette.

The Divine Image (William Blake)

To Mercy, Pity, Peace, and Love,
All pray in their distress:
And to these virtues of delight
Return their thankfulness.

For Mercy, Pity, Peace, and Love,
Is God, our father dear:
And Mercy, Pity, Peace, and Love,
Is Man, his child and care.

For Mercy has a human heart,
Pity, a human face:
And Love, the human form divine,
And Peace, the human dress.

Then every man of every clime,
That prays in his distress,
Prays to the human form divine,
Love, Mercy, Pity, Peace.

And all must love the human form,
In heathen, Turk, or Jew.
Where Mercy, Love, & Pity dwell,
There God is dwelling too.

Vorwort

In jeder Religion werden die gleichen Tugenden beschrieben und dargestellt. Religionskriege haben uns gezeigt, dass, wie im deutschen Grundgesetz beschrieben, es eine Religionsfreiheit geben darf. Jeder soll auch seine Religion oder nicht Religion leben. Juden, Muslime und Christen teilen die hebräische Bibel (bzw. Teile davon) als gemeinsames religiöses Werk, wobei sie in den jeweiligen Traditionen unterschiedliche Namen und Interpretationen hat. Konkret handelt es sich um die Tora im Judentum, die Tawrat im Islam und die Bibel im Christentum.

Als Christ mit großer Offenheit zum Buddhismus und all den anderen Religionen hat mich das Universum oder der liebe Gott mit der Eingebung erfreut mal in Gedichtform die für mich schönsten Passagen der Bibel und buddhistischen Schriften in der Musik der Sprache zu zeichnen.

Das größte Gut der Christen ist nach christlichem Verständnis die Liebe – besonders die Liebe zu seinem Nächsten. Dies basiert auf den zentralen Lehren Jesu Christi, insbesondere dem Doppelgebot der Liebe, wie es in Matthäus 22,37-40 formuliert ist.

Foreword

The same virtues are described and portrayed in every religion. Religious wars have shown us that, as described in the German Basic Law, religious freedom is permissible. Everyone should practice their own religion or non-religion. Jews, Muslims, and Christians share the Hebrew Bible (or parts of it) as a common religious work, although it has different names and interpretations in the respective traditions. Specifically, these are the Torah in Judaism, the Tawrat in Islam, and the Bibel in Christianity.

As a Christian with great openness to Buddhism and all other religions, the universe, or rather God, has graced me with the inspiration to depict in poem form what I consider to be the most beautiful passages of the Bible and Buddhist scriptures in the music of language.

According to Christian understanding, the greatest good of Christians is love—especially love for one's neighbor. This is based on the central teachings of Jesus Christ, in particular the double commandment of love, as formulated in Matthew 22:37-40.

Friedenssuche (Petrus 3)

Wer das Leben liebt, die Tage wunderschön,
der hüte seine Zunge, lass Böses vergeh'n.
Die Lippen rein, kein Trug soll klingen,
nur Wahrheit soll ihr Lied besingen.

Vom Bösen wend' dich ab, tu Gutes gern,
im Herzen trag' die Liebe, nah und fern.
Such Frieden stets, mit Eifer, mit Macht,
jag ihm nach bei Tag und Nacht.

Denn Frieden ist's, der Seelen erhellt,
ein Gut, das die Welt zusammenhält.
Im Tun des Guten, im Reden klar,
wird Leben zur Freude, so wunderbar.

Pursuit of Peace (Petrus 3)

Whoever cherishes life's radiant days,
Must guard their tongue from evil's ways.
Let lips stay pure, let no deceit arise,
Only truth should echo in their cries.

Turn away from wrong, embrace the good with cheer,
Hold love close, both far and near.
Seek peace with your heart, chase it through the night,
With steadfast love, pursue its holy light.

For peace alone can make the spirit glow,
A treasure binding all the world up and below.
In deeds of kindness, words of clarity spun,
Life blooms with joy and happiness done.

Psalm 1

Wohl dem, der wandert weg vom bösen Rat,
der nicht den Pfad der Sünder geht zur Tat,
der weit weg vom Kreis der Spötter sitzt und lacht,
sondern im Herzen des Herrn sein Glück erwacht.

Sein Sinn erfreut sich am Gesetz des Lichts,
er sinnt bei Tag und Nacht des stillen Pflichts,
wie ein Baum, der am Bache steht,
der Frucht in seiner Zeit voll Reife geht.

Sein Blatt verwelkt nicht, grün in jeder Zeit,
sein Tun gelingt, im Segen eingereiht.
Doch anders die, die Gottlosigkeit ergreift,
wie Spreu, vom Winde fortgeweht, zerstreift.

Im Gericht finden sie keinen festen Grund,
die Sünder sind nicht im Gerechten Bund.
Der Herr erkennt den Pfad der Reinen klar.
Unlauterer Weg führt tief ins Verderben, wohl wahr.

Psalm 1

Blessed is the man, who does not walk with evil vision,
who does not follow the path of sinners to action,
who does not sit and laugh in the circle of mockers,
but whose happiness awakens in the heart of God.

His mind delights in the law of light,
in quiet duty he meditates day and night,
like a tree that stands by a stream of water,
which bears fruit in its full season to cater.

It's leaf does not wither, green at all time callings,
his deeds prosper, ranked among blessings.
But it is different for those whom wickedness wins,
like chaff blown by the wind, scattered in sins.

In judgment they find no firm foundation,
sinners not in the righteous consolation.
The Lord clearly recognizes the path of the pure.
The wicked way leads to deep destruction for sure.

Psalm 5

Dem Vorsänger, mit Flötenspiel erklingt,
Ein Psalm von David, der zum Himmel singt.
Vernimm, o Herr, mein Wort, mein sanftes Flehen,
Achte auf mein Seufzen, hör mein Wehen!

Mein König, mein Gott, zu dir erhebt sich mein Gebet,
In der Frühe hörst du meine Stimme, klar und unverdreht.
Ich stehe bereit, blicke auf zu deinem Thron,
Dein Licht bei Anbruch der Dämmerung schon.

Denn du liebst nicht, was gesetzlos ist und trügt,
Der Böse findet bei dir keine Ruh, denn er lügt.
Prahler und Täter des Unrechts vor Gericht,
Lügner vertilgst du, Falsche scheuen dein Licht.

Doch durch deine Gnade tret ich ein in dein Haus,
Im heiligen Tempel bete ich, gebe Ehrfurcht und Braus.
Leite mich, Herr, in deiner Gerechtigkeit,
Um meiner Feinde willen, ebne mir die Wahrhaftigkeit.

Ihr Mund birgt Lügen, ihr Herz ist Bosheit rein,
Ihr Rachen ein Grab, heuchelt mit falschem Schein.
Sprich sie schuldig, laß sie fallen durch ihr Tun,
Verstoße sie, denn sie empörten sich gegen deinen Ton.

Doch jubeln sollen, die auf dich vertrauen stets,
Ewiglich frohlocken, von dir beschirmt und gesegnet.
Die deinen Namen lieben, in dir finden sie Glück,
Denn du segnest den Gerechten mit Gnade, du gibst
es zurück

Psalm 5

To the cantor, accompanied by flute playing,
A psalm of David to heaven singing
Hear, O Lord, my word, my gentle supplication.
Attend to my sigh, hear my ululation!

My King, my God, to you rises my prayer.
In the morning you hear my voice, clear and truth sayer.
I stand ready, looking up to your throne,
your light is the eternity tone.

For you do not love what is lawless and deceitful.
The wicked finds no rest in you because he is distrustful.
Boasters and wrongdoers in the courtroom.
You destroy liars, and this pitiful doom.

But by your grace I enter your house in analogy,
to the holy temple I pray, giving reverence and eulogy.
Guide me, Lord, in your righteousness to see.
For the sake of my enemies, make truth clear to me.

Their mouths conceal lies, their hearts are pure in
wickedness.
Their throats are graves, feigning deceit witness.
Condemn them, let them fall by their deeds.
Cast them away and take what it needs.

But those who trust in you shall always rejoice,
Eternally exult, protected and blessed by your voice.
Those who love your name will find happiness.
For you bless the righteous with mercy and success.

Universale Liebe (Matthäus 19)

Am Anfang schuf der Herr das Paar,
Mann und Frau, so wunderbar.
Er sprach: „Verlasst nun Heim und Hort,
find't zueinander, werdet eins am Ort."

Zwei Herzen, die sich fest verbinden,
ein Fleisch, ein Bund, im Ewig finden.
Was Gott in Liebe hat vereint,
da es im Himmelslicht scheint.

Ein Weg, ein Leben, Hand in Hand,
im göttlichen Willen fest verwandt.
Nicht zwei, nein, eins in Herz und Sinn,
so führt die Liebe stets zum Ziel hin.

United love (Matthew 19)

In the dawn of time, the Lord did weave,
A man, a woman, His heart's reprieve.
"Leave your past, your home, your kin,"
He spoke, "and let your life together begin."

Two souls entwined, their spirits blend,
One flesh, one love, no end to mend.
Bound by grace in sacred vow,
No hand of man shall part them now.

Hand in hand, they walk as one,
Through divine will, a bond is done.
Heart and mind in union sweet,
Love's true path makes life complete.

Die Heilung eines Gelähmten (Lukas 5)

Im Lande weit, nach Tagen fern,
Kehrt er zurück, des Herrn's Stern,
Im Haus versammelt, dicht gedrängt das Volk,
Kein Platz mehr draußen, ein leiser Erfolg.

Das Wort er sprach, erfüllt von Licht,
Da kamen sie, ein krankes Gesicht,
Ein Gelähmter, von vieren getragen,
Durch Menge hindurch, ein Weg voll Fragen.

Durch das Dach die Liegematte gesenkt,
Glaube erstrahlt, wo Hoffnung geschenkt,
Jesus sah hin, ihr Herz so rein,
Sprach: „Sohn, dir sind Sünden vergeben, sei fein!"

Die Schriftgelehrten, im Herzen erbittert,
„Wer kann vergeben, nur Gott ist gesittet?"
Doch Jesus erkannte ihr stilles Gedenken,
Fragte: „Warum zankt ihr, was ist leichter zu denken?"

„Sünd' vergeben oder aufstehen befehlen?
Seht nun die Macht, die ich und Gott für euch wählen!"
Zu dem Gelähmten, mit fester Hand,
„Steh auf, nimm deine Matte, geh in das Land!"

Und sogleich erhob er sich, stark und klar,
Nahm seine Last, ging hinaus, wunderbar,

Die Menge staunte, pries Gott im Chor,
„So etwas sahen wir nie zuvor!"

Ein Wunder erblüht, der Glaube erwacht,
Im Lande lebt Hoffnung, die die Runde macht,
Der Sohn des Menschen, mit Macht gesandt,
Heilt Leib und Seele, ein göttliches Pfand.

The Healing of a Paralytic (Luke 5)

Across a far land, after days away,
He returned, the Lord's star to pray.
Gathered in the house, the people crowded together,
No room outside, a quiet success, this get together.

The word he spoke, filled with light in space.
There they came, a sick face,
A paralytic, carried by four with ambitions
Through the crowd, a path full of questions.

Through the roof, the mat lowered,
Faith shines where hope is given and empowered
Jesus looked, their hearts so pure,
Said: "Son, your sins are forgiven, be assure!"

The scribes, their hearts embittered,
"Who can forgive, only God glittered?"
But Jesus recognized their silent remembrance,
Asked: "Why do you quarrel? What to enhence?"

"Forgive sins or command them to rise?
Now see the power that I and God choose to arise!" To
the paralyzed man, with a firm hand,
"Stand up, take your mat, go into the land!"

And immediately he rose, strong and clear,
Took his burden, went forth, miraculously here,

The crowd marveled, praising God in chorus core,
"We have never seen anything like this before!"

A miracle blossoms, faith awakens in record.
Hope lives in the land, spreading the word,
The Son of Man, sent with strength,
Heals body and soul, with divine length.

Frucht des Geistes (Galater 5)

Des Geistes Frucht, so reich und klar,
die Liebe, im Herzen rein und wahr.
Freude sprudelt, hell gar tausendfach,
Friede ruht in der Seele Gemach.

Geduld erblüht in stiller Zeit,
Freundlichkeit strahlt, macht Herzen weit.
Güte wärmt, gibt Trost und Kraft,
Treue hält, was ewig schafft.

Sanftmut spricht in leisen Tönen,
Keuschheit lässt die Seele erschönen.
Kein Gesetz kann je verwehren,
Was der Geist uns will gewähren.

Fruit of the Spirit (Galatians 5)

The Spirit's fruit, so radiant, so pure,
Is love, deep-rooted, steadfast, sure.
Joy, a fountain, sparkles clear and bright,
Peace, a haven, calms the soul's soft night.

In silent moments, patience gently grows,
Kindness beams, where tender mercy flows.
Goodness warms, a balm of strength and grace,
Faithfulness endures, eternal in its place.

With gentle whispers, softness shapes the heart,
Chastity adorns the soul with sacred art.
No law can bind what Spirit freely gives,
In these sweet fruits, the soul forever lives.

Jesu Macht über die bösen Geister und die Lästerung (Markus)

In ein Haus trat er, die Menge drängte sacht,
So dicht das Brot im Mund verlor sein Gewicht,
Die Seinen kamen, wollten ihn umfangen,
„Er ist von Sinnen!" – ihre Urteile klangen.

Doch Schriftgelehrte, aus Jerusalem herab,
Sprachen giftig: „Beelzebul ist sein Trab!"
„Durch des Dämons Fürst treibt er sie fort,"
Ihr Argwohn wuchs im finsteren Wort.

Da rief er sie, in Gleichnissen so klar,
„Wie kann der Satan sich selbst vertreiben, gar?
Ein Reich, entzweit, zerfällt in Staub und Wind,
Ein Haus gespalten, wo bleibt sein Sinn?"

„Der Starke gebunden, sein Haus beraubt,
Erst dann wird sein Hort im Sturm geraubt.
Vergebung sei den Sünden, die man spricht,
Doch wer den Heiligen Geist lästert, fällt ins Nichts."

Ein ewiges Gericht, kein Gnadenblick,
Denn unrein nannten sie den Geist so sacht,
Die Wahrheit brach durch ihre falschen Zungen,
Jesu Macht siegte, wo Hass sich drängt.

Die Menge staunte, die Finsternis erlag,
Sein Wort ein Licht, das keinen Schatten mag,
Über Dämonen herrscht er, stark und rein,
Doch wehe, wer den Heil'gen Geist vernein't.

Jesus' Power Over Evil Spirits
and Blasphemy (Mark)

He stepped within a house, the throng pressed near,
Bread in his mouth grew light, its weight unclear.
His followers surged, their arms outstretched to hold,
Yet cries arose: "His mind is lost!" they told.

From Jerusalem's heights, the scribes descended,
Their words like venom, sharp and unamended.
"Beelzebul's his guide!" they hissed with scorn,
"By demon's prince, his miracles are born."

He called them close, with parables profound:
"How can Satan's own hand his throne confound?
A kingdom split will crumble, turn to dust,
A house divided falls, its strength unjust."

"The strong man bound, his treasures swept away,
His house is plundered in the storm's fierce sway.
All sins may find forgiveness, soft and free,
But blasphemy against the Spirit shall not be."

No mercy waits for those who name it vile,
Who cloak the truth in dark deceit and guile.
The Spirit's light, unshadowed, pierced their claim,
And Jesus' power burned through hatred's flame.

The crowd stood awed, as darkness fell apart,
His word a beacon kindling every heart.
O'er demons strong, his holy strength endures,
Yet woe to those, who shun the Spirit lectures.

Das Licht auf dem Leuchter (Markus)

Er sprach zu ihnen, mit klarer Stimm',
„Kommt das Licht, um verborgen zu glimm'n?
Unter Scheffel oder Bett soll es ruh'n,
Oder strahlt es hell, auf Leuchter zu tun?"

Denn nichts bleibt verborgen, im Schatten verstaubt,
Was heimlich geschieht, wird offenbar erlaubt,
Wer Ohren hat, der höre die Mahnung,
Laßt das Licht erstrahlen, in stiller Ehrung.

„Achtet, was ihr hört, mit wachem Sinn,
Mit dem Maß ihr gebt, wird euch zum Gewinn.
Wer teilt, dem wird gegeben, im Überfluss,
Wer hält zurück, verliert, was er besitzt, bewusst."

Ein Ruf ergeht, die Weisheit zu tragen,
Das Licht der Wahrheit soll alle Wege wagen,
Auf Leuchtern hoch, für alle sichtbar sein,
Ein Segen für jene, die lauschen, weise und rein.

The Light on the Lampstand (Mark)

With voice serene, he spoke to all,
"Does light in secret softly fall?
Beneath a bushel, under bed, does it hide?
Or raised on high, does it shine wide?"

No secret lingers, cloaked in shade,
Nor deed in darkness stays unmade.
What's veiled in silence shall be shown,
In open light, the truth made be known.

Let ears awake, his warning hear,
In quiet awe, let hearts revere.
The light of truth, unyielding, bright,
Shall pierce the gloom and banish night.

"Take heed," he said, "with mindful care,
The measure given shapes what's fair.
To those who share, more shall be sent,
But those who hoard find all in the end."

A call resounds, wisdom to bear,
Through paths of truth, let light declare.
On lampstands high, for all to see,
Blessed are those, who hear with glee.

Das Hohelied der Liebe (Korinther 13)

Wenn ich in Zungen der Menschen und Engel sing',
Doch Liebe mir fehlt, bin ich nur Klang, der erkling',
Ein tönendes Erz, eine klingende Schelle im Wind,
Ohne Herz, das liebt, bleibt mein Wort ungesinnt.

Weissag' ich Geheimnisse, kennt' alle Welt,
Versetz' ich Berge, voll Glauben erhellt,
Doch Liebe nicht in mir, bin ich Staub, ein Nichts,
Ein Schatten, der verblasst, Teil des kühlen Lichts.

Gäb' ich mein Gut, mein Leben gäbe preis,
Ohne Liebe nützt's nichts, verhallt in Schweigen leis'.
Die Liebe ist geduldig, gütig, sanft und rein,
Sie neidet nicht, sie prahlt nicht, sie ist kein Schein.

Unanständig ist sie nicht, sucht nicht ihren Gewinn,
Erbittert sich nicht, rechnet Böses nicht hinein.
Sie freut sich nicht am Unrecht, da Wahrheit sie erhellt,
Erträgt alles, glaubt alles, hofft, wo Hoffnung zerfällt.

Die Liebe hört nie auf, ein ewiges Band,
Weissagung vergeht, Sprachen schweigen im Land,
Erkenntnis schwindet, Stückwerk fällt dahin,
Wenn Vollkommenheit kommt, wird es ein Neubeginn.

Ein Kind sprach kindlich, dachte kindlich, so sein Urteil,
Als Mann vergaß ich, was meinem Geist wurde Teil.

Im Spiegel ein Rätsel, ein Bild im Zwielicht,
Doch dann im Angesicht, erkannt im hellen Licht.

Glaube, Hoffnung, Liebe, drei Säulen bestehen,
Doch größer ist die Liebe, die wir begehen.
Ein Lied, das ewig singt, durch Raum und Zeit,
es singt in den Tönen unserer Menschlichkeit.

The Song of Love (Corinthians 13)

Though I speak with tongues of men and angels' grace,
Without love, I'm but a hollow in echoing space,
A clanging ore, a acute and bluster din,
My words, unmoored by love, hold no meaning within.

Though I unravel mysteries, the world's secrets unfold,
Though faith moves mountains, steadfast, firm, and bold,
Without love's fire, I am naught but dust,
A fading shadow, lost in twilight's rust.

If I give all I own, cast my life to the flame,
Without love's truth, my deeds dissolve in shame.
Love is patient, kind, a gentle, steady stream,
It envies not, nor boasts, nor chases hollow dreams.

It shuns disgrace, seeks not its own desire,
Holds no bitterness, counts no wrongs in ire.
Bears all, believes, and hopes where frail hopes die.
Injustice brings no joy, but truth lifts up high,

Love never falters, an eternal, woven thread,
when prophecies grow dim and mortal tongues fall dead.
Knowledge is a part of understanding
Perception a patient longing.

As children, we spoke with childish thought and rhyme,
But as grown older I dismissed that time.
Through the mirror we see the dark picture
face to face in forming our nature.

Faith, hope, and love, three pillars forever stand,
But love is the greatest within this holy band.
A song eternal, soaring through time and space,
Love, the boundless light, our dream and saving grace.

Freundschaft (Römer 1)

Ein Sehnen tief im Herzen ruht,
Euch zu begegnen, das ist gut.
Gottes Geschenke, reich und klar,
Teil' ich mit euch, so wunderbar.

Gestärkt sollt ihr durch Liebe sein,
Im Glauben wachsen, nicht allein.
Gemeinsam, Hand in Hand, vereint,
Wo Mut und Hoffnung neu erscheint.

Wenn ich bei euch, im Kreise steh',
Im Glauben wachsen wir, oh seh'!
Einander stützen, Herz an Herz,
Im Licht des Glaubens, frei von Schmerz.

Friendship (Romans 1)

A yearning deep within my soul does lie,
To meet you face to face beneath the sky.
God's gifts, so radiant, pure, and bright,
I share with you, a wondrous light.

Through love's embrace, your strength shall grow,
In faith you'll rise, no longer solo.
Hand in hand, together we stand,
Where hope and courage bloom, expand.

Among you all, in circle's grace,
Our faith shall soar, we'll find our place.
Heart to heart, we lift each other high,
In faith's pure light, where pain does die.

Die Geisteswirkungen zur Erbauung (Korinther)

Strebt nach der Liebe, ein helles Geleit,
Doch eifert auch nach Geisteswirkungen, seid bereit,
Am meisten sehnt euch nach Weissagung,
Denn sie erhebt die Gemeinde zum Lobgesang.

Wer in Sprachen spricht, für Gott allein,
Geheimnisse flüstert, im Geist so fein,
Doch wer weissagt, erbaut, ermahnt, tröstet klar,
Die Gemeinde wächst, wo Weisheit sich paart.

Ich wünsch', ihr sprächet alle in Zungen frei,
Doch größer noch, wenn ihr weissagt dabei,
Denn Weisheit übertrifft, wenn sie gedeutet wird,
Erbauung schenkt, wo das Herz sich fügt als Hirt'.

Kommt ich mit Sprachen, was nützt es euch denn,
Ohne Offenbarung, Erkenntnis, als Leuchtturm brenn.
Wie Flöte oder Harfe, mit klarem Klang,
leuchten darf die Botschaft, nicht nur erklingen im Gang.

Betet mit Geist, doch auch mit Verstand,
Lobsingt mit Herz, was die Seele erkannt,
Sonst bleibt der Unkundige in seinem Rahmen,
Kein Bau geschieht, wo kein Sinnessamen.

Fünf Worte mit Verstand, die andere lehren,
Sind mehr als zehntausend, die nur gähren,
Seid nicht kindlich im Denken, sondern rein im Sinn,
Im Verständnis erwachsen, wo Liebe der Gewinn.

Manche Zeichen mögen für Ungläubige sein,
Weissagung für Gläubige ist ein heiliger Schein,
Kommt ein Fremder herein, bei Sprachen verwirrt,
hat sich die göttliche Weissagung entwirrt.

So laßt die Wirkungen zur Gemeinde dienen,
Erbauung seiner Ziele, wo Herzen erschienen,
Mit Liebe und Weisheit, im Einklang geeint,
Ein Chor des Geistes, der ewig sich vereint.

The Workings of the Spirit for Edification (Corinthians)

Pursue love's flame, a radiant guide,
Yet seek the Spirit's gifts, let them abide.
Above all, yearn for prophecy's clear voice,
To lift the church in songs that all rejoice.

Who speaks in tongues communes with God alone,
In mystic whispers, Spirit's breath is sown.
But prophecy builds, exhorts, and comforts true,
The faith grows, where wisdom's light breaks through.

I'd have you all speak tongues with fervent heart,
Yet greater still, let prophecy impart.
For words interpreted bring understanding's gain,
Shepherding souls, where love and truth remain.

What use my tongues if I should come to you,
Without revelation's spark or knowledge true?
Like flute or harp, let notes ring clear and bright,
A message shining and not lost in endless night.

Pray with the spirit, but with mind awake,
Sing praises heartfelt, for the soul's own sake.
Yet the unknowing stand mute at Amen's call,
No growth takes root, where sense finds no hall.

Five words of wisdom, shared to guide and teach,
Outweigh ten thousand tongues that merely preach.
Be not as children in thought, but pure in mind,
Mature in love, where understanding is kind.

Let tongues be signs for those who doubt the way,
But prophecy's light for believers' unswerving stay.
A stranger, lost in tongues, may turn aside,
Yet prophecy calls their heart to God's own tide.

Let gifts uplift the faith in unity's embrace,
Edification the goal where hearts find grace.
In love and wisdom, joined as one we stand,
A choir of Spirit, bound in eternal band.

Streben nach Frieden (Petrus 3)

Wer das Leben liebt, die Tage heiter,
Hüte seine Zunge, spreche Worte weiter.
Kein böses Reden, kein Trug soll sein,
Die Lippen rein, voll Wahrheit fein.

Vom Pfad des Bösen wende dich weg,
Tu Gutes, liebe, pflanze Glück im Steg.
Den Frieden suche, mit Herz und Macht,
Jag ihm nach durch des Lebens Nacht.

Im Tun des Guten, mit reinem Wort,
Blüht Leben auf am seligen Ort.
Frieden, der Seele sanftes Licht,
Führt zum Glück in Gottes Gesicht.

Path for Peace (Peter 3)

Who loves life's glow, its days so bright,
Must guard their tongue, no words to flight.
No evil spoken, no deceit to weave,
Pure lips let truth's sweet song achieve.

From evil's path, turn swift away,
Sow good, spread love, let joy hold sway.
With heart and power, seek peaceful grace,
Chase it through life's darkened space.

In doing good, with words sincere,
Life blooms where blessings blossom near.
Peace, the soul's soft radiant beam,
Guides to joy in God's eternal gleam.

Die unerforschlichen Wege Gottes (Hiob)

Sieh, erhaben thront er in mächt'ger Kraft,
Wer lehrt wie Gott und erkennt Meisterschaft?
Wer fragt ihn kühn, wer tadelt sein Tun,
Sein Weg so tief, ein ewiger Ruhm?

Erheb dein Herz, sing sein gewalt'ges Werk, gern
Das Menschenaug' erblickt es, von weit und fern,
So hoch er ist, wir kennen ihn nicht ganz,
Sein Lebensjahr ein Rätsel, ein heil'ger Tanz.

Wassertropfen zieht er empor, ein Wunder,
Regen fließt herab, nährt Strom und Kunder,
Die Wolken brechen auf, spenden reichen Segen,
Auf Völker nieder, ein himmlisches Pflegen.

Verstehst du, wie Wolken sich spannen,
Wie Donner rollt, sein Zelt bemannen.
Sein Licht erstrahlt, bedeckt des Meeres Sand,
Mit Blitz und Macht regiert er jedes Land.

Speise spendet er, die Fülle in der Hand,
Sein Blitzstrahl zückt, gehorcht dem hohen Band,
Der Donner kündet, selbst das Vieh erblickt,
Sein Heranziehen, wo die Erde sich bückt.

Unerforschlich sind seine Pfade, so rein,
Ein Schöpferthron, jenseits mein und dein,

In Ehrfurcht neigen wir uns, dem göttlichen Flügel,
des Herrn's Wege bleiben ewig, wie heil'ge Hügel.

The Unsearchable Ways of God (Job)

Behold him, throned in might, where power reigns,
Who teaches like our Lord, who breaks all chains?
Who dares to question, or defy his deeds,
His paths unfathomable, his glory succeeds?

Lift up your heart, sing gladly of his might,
His works resplendent in all human sight.
Though lofty, his essence we can't trace,
His years a riddle, a sacred dance though space.

He gathers water's drops, a wondrous feat,
Rain pours to nurture streams where life's waves meet.
Clouds burst with blessings, gifts from heavens' care,
Bestowed on peoples, boundless love to share.

Can you grasp how clouds unfold their span,
Or thunder's roar within his mighty plan?
His light illumes, across the sea's wide sand,
With lightning's flash, he rules over every land.

Abundance flows, his generous hand provides,
His lightning dances where his will presides.
Thunder heralds, even cattle sense his call,
His presence bends the earth where mortals fall.

His ways, inscrutable, in purity abide,
A creator's throne, no mortal can deride.
We bow in awe, beneath his holy wings,
The Lord's eternal paths, where glory sings.

Barmherzigkeit (Matthäus 9)

Nun geht, und denkt darüber nach, was das bedeutet,
wenn man Barmherzigkeit einläutet.
Weder Opfer noch Täter sein
Die Gnade wirken lassen im Sonnenschein.

Dann versteht ihr auch, dass ich nicht gekommen bin, die
Gerechten zu rufen, sondern die Sünder im Sinn.
Sie sind es, die es zu retten gilt, hier auf Erden
auf das sie einst geläutert werden.

Mercy (Matthew 9)

Now go and think about what it means
to usher in compassion by all means.
To be neither victim nor perpetrator
To let grace work with the shining mediator.

Then you will also understand that I have not come
to call the righteous, but sinners in mind.
They are the ones who must be saved here on out home
so that they may one day reach maturity behind.

Das Stellvertretende Leiden des Messias (Jesaja)

Wer glaubt unserer Kunde, wer sieht den Arm des Herrn
gelassen?
Ein Schößling spross aus dürrem Land, in Stille nur geboren,
Kein Glanz, kein Anblick, der uns zog, verachtet, verlassen,
Ein Mann der Schmerzen, tief im Leid, vor uns verborgen.

Er trug unsre Krankheit, lud Schmerzen auf sich,
Wir hielten ihn für geschlagen, von Gott geplagt und fern,
Doch durchbohrt um unsre Schuld, zerschlagen um
Vergeben leidlich,
Sein Schmerz brachte Frieden, seine Wunden heilten gern.

Wie Schafe irrten wir, ein jeder seinen Weg
Doch auf ihn warf der Herr unsre Schuld, so schwer,
Er schwieg wie ein Lamm zur Schlacht, ohne Schreck
In Drangsal fortgenommen, sein Gang mit Ehr.

Für ihre Übertretungen sein Grab, bei Reichen sein Tod,
Kein Unrecht in seinem Mund, kein Trug, nur Licht,
Dem Herrn gefiel es, ihn zu brechen, in seiner Not,
Sein Leben ein Schuldopfer, eine heilige Pflicht.

Nach Mühsal sah er Lust, Nachkommenschaft erblühte,
Seine Tage wuchsen, das Werk des Herrn gelang,
Durch seine Weisheit macht er viele gerecht mit Güte,
Trägt ihre Sünden, ein Erlöser, stark und bang.

Die Ungerechtigkeiten der Vielen gab der Herr ihm zum Erbteil,
Starke nahm er mit Würde, sein Opfer so rein,
Durch ihn wurde Übertretern seine Fürbitte zu Teil.
Für Übeltäter betete er, ein König im Sonnenschein.

The Vicarious Suffering of the Messiah (Isaiah)

Yet he was wounded for our transgressions,
he was bruised for our ignorant iniquities.
The chastisement of our peace was upon his missions,
and he are healed us and rose our abilities.

He took our ailments, bore our grief's heavy load,
We deemed him stricken, cursed by God, alone he strode.
Yet pierced for our faults, crushed for our sin's decree,
His wounds brought peace, his stripes our healing's key.

Like wayward sheep, we strayed on paths apart,
But God laid all our guilt upon his burdened heart.
He beared it with a loving grace,
and with a composed face.

His grave among the wicked, his death with wealth's
embrace,
No falsehood on his lips, no shadow of disgrace.
The Lord ordained his pain, a sacrifice divine,
His life a pure offering to cleanse the sins of time.

Through toil, he saw joy, his seed in glory grew,
His days extended, God's will shining through.
By wisdom's light, he justified the scenery and throng,
Bearing their sins, a redeemer, steadfast and strong.

The Lord bestowed on him a countless heritage,
The mighty as his spoil, his sacrifice being sage.
He faced death's sting, among transgressors cast,
Yet prayed for sinners, a king whose love will last.

Zufriedenheit (Philipper 4:13)

In Armut leb' ich, still und klar,
Im Überfluss, so wunderbar.
Eingeweiht in jedes Los,
Ob reich, ob arm, der Weg famos.

Satt sein weiß ich, Hunger spür' ich,
Mangel kenn' ich, Überfluss führ' ich.
In Gelassenheit, da ruht mein Herz,
In allen Lagen frei von Schmerz.

Denn ob ich habe, ob ich brauch',
es ist der bewegte Lebenshauch'.
Durch den, der mich stark macht
kann ich allem begegnen mit Pracht.

Contentment (Philippians 4:13)

In poverty I live, quiet and clear,
In abundance considerately dear.
Initiated into every lot,
Whether rich or poor, the way is glorious.

I know being full, I feel hunger,
I know lack, as well as abundance.
In calmness, there my heart rests,
free spirit in all situations, the best.

For whether I have or need,
the moving breath of life succeeds.
Through Him who makes me courageous
I can face everything with splendor continuous.

Geistliche Haltung in Bedrängnissen
(Der erste Brief des Apostels Petrus)

Seid gleichgesinnt, voll Mitgefühl und Zart,
Mit brüderlicher Liebe, barmherzig und klug im Start,
Vergeltet Böses nicht mit gleichem Schlag,
Sondern segnet, denn Segen ist euer Beitrag.

Wer Leben liebt, wer gute Taten sucht,
Bewahre Zunge vor Trug, die Lippen vor Fluch,
Wend dich vom Bösen ab, tu Gutes mit Mut,
Such Frieden und jage ihm nach, denn er ist gut.

Des Herrn Augen ruh'n auf den Gerechten hier,
Sein Ohr lauscht ihrem Flehen, in heiliger Manier,
Er wendet sich hin zu Freude und Leid,
Das Böse trifft, wo Herzen sind weit.

Wer Gutes will, wem wird Schaden tun?
Leidest du um Gerechtigkeit, bist glücklich nun,
Fürchtet ihr Drohen nicht, stört euch nicht im Sinn,
Heiligt Gott in euren Herzen, ein innerer Gewinn.

Seid bereit, mit Sanftmut Rechenschaft zu geben,
Über Hoffnung, die in euch leuchtet im Leben,
Bewahrt in euch gutes Gewissen, rein und klar,
Laßt Verleumder fallen, ihr Wort unwahr.

Besser leiden für Gut, wenn Gott es will,
Als für Böses büßen, in dunkler Hülle,
In Bedrängnis und Haß steht fest im Licht,
Mit Liebe und Glauben, eine starke Pflicht.

Spiritual Attitude in Times of Affliction
(The First Epistle of the Apostle Peter)

Be one in spirit, with hearts tender and kind,
Bound by love's mercy, with wisdom entwined.
Return not evil with curses that sting,
But bless, for to blessing your soul is pledged to bring.

Who longs for life, for days that are good,
Guard your tongue from deceit, let truth be your food.
Turn from all evil, let courage do right,
Seek peace, pursue it, till it blooms in the light.

The Lord's eyes rest on the just and the true,
His ears open wide to their cries that break through.
Yet His face turns from those who embrace wrong,
For evil consumes where open hearts throng.

Who harms the one who mirrors the good?
If justice brings pain, count it joy where you stood.
Fear not their threats, let your soul remain still,
Sanctify God with a radiant heart's will.

Be ready to answer, with meekness and grace,
For the hope that within you lights up your face.
Keep conscience pure, unclouded, and clear,
Let slanderers' words fall, their shame drawing near.

Better to suffer for good, if God so decree,
Than bear evil's weight in a cloak dark and heavy.
In trials and hate, stand firm in the light,
With love and with faith, fulfill your duty's might.

Neubeginn (Korinther 2)

In Christus' Licht, vereint, erwacht,
Ein neues Sein, in Liebe gebracht.
Das Alte schwindet, verweht im Wind,
Ein neuer Morgen, der Hoffnung find't.

Seht, wie das Neue empor nun steigt,
Die Seele frei, das Herz sich neigt.
Geschaffen neu, in Gnade klar,
das Neue entstand im Ist, fürwahr.

New Beginning (Corinthians 2)

In Christ's light, united with glee,
A new being, brought in love to see.
The old fades, blown away in the wind,
A new morning that finds hope behind.

Look how the new now rises,
A soul free, the heart inclines sunrises.
Created anew, clear in grace,
the new arose on this place.

Der neue Himmel und die neue Erde (Offenbarung)

Ich sah den Himmel neu, die Erde erstand,
Der erste verging, das Meer verlor sein Band,
Johannes erblickte die heilige Stadt,
Ein neues Jerusalem, wie eine Braut im Feigenblatt

Aus Himmelstiefe stieg sie herab,
Gottes Zelt bei den Menschen, ein heiliger Pfad,
Eine Stimme rief laut, erfüllt von Licht,
„Sein Volk wird er sein, ihr Gott in der Mit."

Er wischt die Tränen, der Tod schweigt still,
Kein Leid, kein Schmerz, kein Weh mehr will,
Vom Thron ertönte: „Sieh, alles neu!"
Wahrhaftige Worte, sein Bund, bleibt treu.

„Ich bin das A und das O, Anfang und Ziel,
Dem Dürstenden schenk ich Lebensziel,
Wer überwindet, erbt alles, mein Sohn,
Mein Gott wird er sein, in ewigem Ton."

Doch Feigheit und Lügen, Unzucht und Haß,
Götzendienst, Mord, in finst'rem Nass,
Ihr Teil ist der See, Feuer und Schwefel brennt,
Der zweite Tod, wo Hoffnung sich trennt.

Ein neues Reich erstrahlt, rein und klar,
Gottes Liebe siegt, ein leuchtender Star,

Die Erde erneuert, der Himmel so weit,
wo Gerechtigkeit lebt in jeder Zeit.

The New Heaven and the New Earth (Revelation)

I saw the heavens anew, the earth arose.
The first passed away, the sea lost its bond.
John beheld the holy city.
A new Jerusalem, like a bride in a fig leaf.

From the depths of heaven she descended,
God's tent with men, a holy path.
A voice cried out loudly, filled with light,
"He will be his people, their God with us."

He wipes away tears, death remains silent.
No more suffering, no more pain, no more woe.
From the throne came the cry: "Behold, all things are new!"
True words, a covenant that remains faithful.

"I am the Alpha and the Omega, beginning and end.
To the thirsty I give the fountain of life.
He who overcomes inherits all things, my son.
He will be my God, in an everlasting voice."

But cowardice and lies, fornication and hatred,
Idolatry and murder, in the dark waters,
Their portion is the lake, fire and brimstone burn,
The second death, where hope then separates.

A new kingdom shines, pure and clear,
God's love triumphs, a shining star,
The earth renewed, the sky so wide,
In eternity rests where justice cries out.

Vom Richten (Matthäus, Vers 7)

Richtet nicht, dass ihr nicht gerichtet werdet
Denn wie ihr urteilt, so wird's euch gemessen.
Mit welchem Maß ihr misst, kehrt's zu euch zurück,
Ein Spiegel des Herzens, im göttlichen Ermessen.

Warum siehst du den Splitter im Auge des Bruders
Doch übersiehst den Balken, dein Blick ist woanders
Wie sagst du: „Warte, ich helf' dir, den Splitter zu ziehn,"
Wenn ein Balken dein eigenes Auge bedeckt mit Mühn'?

Du Heuchler, wirf erst den Balken hinaus,
Klar dein Blick, reinige dein eigenes Haus.
Dann siehst du klar, mit sanftem Verstand,
Und nimmst den Splitter aus Bruders Hand.

On Judging (Matthew, verse 7)

Judge not, lest judgment find your heart,
For as you weigh, so fate will part.
The measure you give, the scale you wield,
Returns to you in truth revealed.

Why spy the speck in another's sight,
Yet miss the beam that clouds your light?
You haste to mend their flaw so small,
While your own shadow blinds your call.

Hypocrite, first cast out the beam,
Let clarity flow, a cleansing stream.
With gentle mind and vision clear,
Then guide the speck with tender care.

Die Weisheit bewahrt vor bösen Wegen (Sprüche)

Mein Sohn, nimm meine Worte auf, bewahre sie im Leben,
Leih deinem Ohr der Weisheit Klang, gib deinem Herz
ein Streben,
Flehe um Verstand, such Einsicht wie ein Schatz,
und herrliche Erkenntnis erhält ihren Platz.

Aus Gottes Mund strömt Weisheit, klar und rein,
Er schützt den Aufrichtigen, sein Pfad so fein,
Für Lauterkeit bereitet er Gelingen und Ruh,
Bewahrt das Recht, behütet die Getreuen immerzu.

Wenn Weisheit in dein Herz sich senkt, so süß, gelöst
Wird Besonnenheit dich schirmen, Einsicht dich erlöst,
Von bösen Wegen, falschen Zungen fern,
Von krummen Pfaden, wo Finsternis sich wendet gern.

Die sich im Bösen freuen, Verkehrtheit lieben,
Ihre Wege trügerisch, im Abgrund treiben,
Die Verführerin lockt mit glatter Rede weit,
Ihr Haus führt zum Tod, kein Leben mehr in Zeit.

Wandle auf Wegen der Guten, halte fest,
Auf Pfaden der Gerechten, im Licht gepresst,
Die Redlichen bewohnen das Land, so klar,
Die Gottlosen vergehen, vertrieben, verloren, gar.

Die Weisheit sei dein Schild, dein Leitstern hell,
Ein Pfad zum Leben, wo Liebe sich erhellt,
Im Streben nach dem Guten, im Herzen rein,
Bewahrt vor Finsternis, ein heiliger Schein.

Wisdom Protects from Evil Ways (Proverbs)

My son, embrace my words, let them take root,
Hold fast their truth, let them bear fruit.
Lend your ear to wisdom's gentle call,
Give your heart to striving, surrender all.

Seek understanding, chase insight's gleam,
Like hidden treasure in a radiant dream.
From God's mouth flows wisdom, pure and bright,
A shield for the just, a guide through the night.

He paves success for those with honest hearts,
Upholds the faithful, guards them from false starts.
When wisdom settles deep within your soul,
Its sweetness calms, makes prudence whole.

Insight redeems, a shield against the dark,
From lying tongues and paths where evil sparks.
From crooked ways where shadows twist and turn,
Where those who love deceit in folly burn.

The temptress calls with words that glide and sway,
Yet her house leads to death, where life decays.
But walk the paths where righteous footsteps tread,
Hold tight to good, by vivid light be led.

The upright dwell in lands of promised peace,
While wicked hearts are banished, lost, decrease.
Let wisdom be your star, your guiding flame,
A path to life where love and truth proclaim.

Maß der Gabe (Lukas 6)

Gib, und reich wird dir's gegeben,
Ein Maß, voll Freude, sprengt dein Leben.
Gedrückt, gerüttelt, überfließend klar,
Füllt Gott den Schoß, so wunderbar.

Mit welchem Maß du misst die Welt,
So wird's dir reichlich zugeteilt.
In Liebe gib, mit offenem Herzen,
Und ernte Segen, frei von Schmerzen.

Measure of the Gift (Luke 6)

Give, and it will be given to your life.
A measure, full of joy, will burst your strife.
Pressed, shaken, overflowing with clarity,
God's womb fills so wonderfully.

With whatever measure you measure the being,
so it will be distributed to you rich in seeing.
Give in love, with an open heart,
And reap blessings, all a part.

Wo man sich raten lässt (Sprüche)

Ein weiser Sohn hört des Vaters Mahnung,
Ein Spötter schließt sein Ohr vor jeder Warnung,
Des Mundes Frucht nährt Gut im Herzen rein,
Doch Treulosigkeit speist sich an Gewalt, so klein.

Wer seinen Mund behütet, schützt sein Leben,
Wer stets ihn öffnet, findet Unglück eben,
Des Faulen Seele giert, doch bleibt sie leer,
Der Fleißige genießt, sein Herz nicht schwer.

Der Gerechte flieht Verleumdung weit,
Der Gottlose schafft Schande, finstres Leid,
Gerechtigkeit bewahrt den Unsträflichen Pfad,
Doch Gottlosigkeit führt den Sünder ins Grab.

Einer prahlt mit Reichtum, hat doch nichts,
Ein Armer birgt viel, in der Stille des Lichts,
Mit Gold kauft mancher sein Leben teuer,
Der Arme sieht das arme Ungeheuer.

Des Gerechten Licht brennt hell und klar,
Des Gottlosen Leuchten erlischt, so gar,
Aus Übermut keimt Streit, ein bitterer Schmerz,
Doch Rat empfangen lässt Weisheit sich entfalten, mit Herz.

Was mühelos kommt, zerrinnt im Wind,
Geduldiges Sammeln mehrt, was der Tag bringt,
Hoffnung, die trügt, macht krank den Geist,
Ein erfüllter Wunsch blüht wie Lebensbaum, zumeist.

Wer das Wort verachtet, geht zugrunde,
Doch Gebot fürchtend, wird er gebunde,
Des Weisen Lehre fließt wie Lebensquelle,
Sie wehrt den Fallstricken, wo Tod sich stellte.

Gute Einsicht schenkt Gunst, ein heller Schein,
Der treulosen Weg ist hart, ein finstrer Stein,
Der Kluge handelt klug, der Tor nur Torheit,
Ein treuer Bote heilt, ein falscher führt ins Leid.

Zucht verachtend sinkt man in Schande tief,
Auf Zurechtweisung hört, kommt man zu Ehr' und Glück,
Verlangen stillt die Seele, ein süßer Frieden,
Vom Bösen weichen ist Toren ein Übel, so schnöden.

Mit Weisen wandern macht weise den Geist,
Mit Narren gehen führt ins Unglück, so heist,
Des Guten Erbe lebt in Kindern und gedeiht.
Das Erbe ist es das alles verzeiht.

Der Ehrenwerte gibt Speise, der Ungerechte raubt,
Das Gute ist es was stehts schafft und erbaut,
Der Gerechte speist satt, der Gottlose hungert,
Wo Rat wohnt, blüht Weisheit, das das Leben verlängert.

Where to Seek Advice (Proverbs)

A wise son heeds his father's guiding voice,
While scoffers shun all warnings, deaf by choice.
The mouth's sweet fruit feeds hearts pure and true,
Yet treachery thrives on violence, bitter and cruel.
Guard well your lips to shield your life from harm,
Loose tongues invite misfortune's reckless charm.
The sluggard craves, yet empty stays his soul,
The diligent reaps, though his heart bears a toll.

The righteous shuns slander's venomous sting,
The wicked weave shame, dark sorrows they bring.
Justice upholds the blameless on their way,
But sin's crooked path leads sinners to decay.
One boasts of riches, yet holds naught but air,
The poor conceal wealth in silence and care.
Gold buys a life, its price so dearly won,
The poor hear no threats, their peace never undone.

The righteous shine with light both clear and bright,
The wicked's lamp fades into endless night.
Arrogance breeds strife, a bitter, piercing pain,
But counsel heeded lets wisdom gently reign.
What's gained with ease dissolves like morning dew,
Yet patient toil builds riches strong and true.
False hope sickens hearts with unfulfilled desire,
Fulfilled wishes bloom, like life's eternal fire.

Who scorns the word will perish in their pride,
But those who fear the law in truth abide.
The wise man's teaching flows, a spring of life,
Deflecting death's cruel snares and mortal strife.

Good insight grants favor, a radiant glow,
The faithless tread a path of hardened woe.
The prudent act with care, the fool with folly,
True messengers heal, while false ones lead to folly.
Spurn discipline, and shame will drag you low,
Heed rebuke, and honor's grace will grow.
Desire fulfilled brings peace, a soul's sweet rest,
To shun evil's path is folly's bitter jest.

Walk with the wise, and wisdom shall you gain,
With fools, misfortune binds you to its chain.
Sinners chase calamity, the righteous find reward,
Goodness endures, while sin's wealth is ignored.

The righteous leave a legacy for their kin,
The sinner's riches scatter in the wind.
New fields feed the just, the unjust steal and roam,
Love guides correction, hate destroys the home.

The righteous eat their fill, their hearts content,
The wicked hunger, their souls forever spent.
Where counsel blooms, there wisdom's light will rise,
A life of truth, where righteousness resides.

Ratschlag (Sprüche 13)

Der arrogante Dummkopf mit den kleinen Ehren
lässt sich nicht belehren
und jeder Versuch, ihn zurecht zu weisen,
endet immer im Streit auf den Lebensgleisen.

Schade wo man sich streitet
und der Mangel an Demut entgleitet.
Im Gegenzug mit Selbsterkenntnis oder der Bereitschaft,
sich etwas sagen zu lassen mit Meisterschaft.

Es ist ein wichtiger Schritt auf dem Weg zur Weisheit, die
eigenen Grenzen zu erkennen mit Achtsamkeit,
Kritik zuzulassen und gute Ratschläge anzunehmen
ist ein interessantes Unternehmen.

Advice (Proverbs 13)

The arrogant fool with little honor
will not be taught, he is not a donor,
and every attempt to correct him with a indice
always ends in a quarrel on the advice.

A pity where beings deeply disagree
the lack of humility we see.
The countermove is self-knowledge, or the willingness
to be told what to do in mastery with awareness.

It is an important step on the path to wisdom
to recognize one's own limitations with freedom.
To accept mindfully criticism and to accept good advice,
is an interesting undertaking, an inner voice.

Reichtum bringt keine Sicherheit (Prediger)

Wer Geld liebt, sehnt sich nach mehr, vergebens, klar
Wer Reichtum jagt, findet keinen Gewinn, wie bizar.
Wo Güter wachsen, da zehren sie schnell,
Der Besitzer sieht nur, was das Auge erhellt.

Süß schlummert der Arbeiter, ob hungrig oder satt,
Der Reiche wälzt sich ruhelos in Überfluss, so platt,
Ein Übel sah ich, Reichtum zum Schaden,
Verloren im Unglück, am Lebensfaden.

Nackt kam er, nackt geht er, kein Erbe im Wind,
Sein Sohn erbt nichts, die Mühe verliert sich im Sinn,
In Finsternis ißt er, Ärger und Zorn sein Teil,
Ein Leben im Schatten, ein müder, schwerer Ziel.

Doch schön ist's, zu essen, zu trinken, zu sein,
Im Licht der Arbeit, die Tage zu weihn,
Ein Teil, den Gott gibt, ein freudiger Lohn,
Denn Reichtum schützt nicht, nur der Liebe Thron.

Wenn Gott Reichtum schenkt, Genuß erlaubt,
Freude im Herzen, die Mühe erlöst, gebaut
Vergißt man die Zeit, im Segen geborgen,
Ein Leben im Frieden, von Gott getragen, zu umsorgen.

Reichtum zerfällt, ein flüchtiger Traum,
Die Arbeit nährt, wo Liebe hat den Raum,

Sicherheit findet, wer sich dem Tag ergibt,
In Gottes Gabe, wo wahres Glück es gibt.

Wealth brings no security (Ecclesiastes)

He who loves gold hungers still, in vain,
Chasing wealth, yet finding no true gain.
Where riches swell, they swiftly fade away,
The owner's eyes see only what decays.

The worker sleeps in peace, with little or much,
While restless wealth lies heavy in its clutch.
I saw an evil—riches turned to harm,
Lost in misfortune, life's fleeting charm.

Naked he came, and naked he departs,
No legacy lingers, no wealth fills the heart.
His son inherits naught, toil's fruit is gone,
In shadows he eats, with wrath his only dawn.

Yet beauty blooms in simple joys of life—
To eat, to drink, to labor free from strife.
God's gift, a portion, brings the heart's reward,
Where love, not wealth, stands sovereign, unmarred.

When God bestows riches, with joy to partake,
The heart finds gladness, redeeming each ache.
Time fades in blessing, sheltered by His grace,
A life of peace, where love holds a main place.

Wealth crumbles swift, a dream that cannot stay,
But work and love sustain the gifted day.
True safety rests in yielding to His care,
Where happiness, God-given, blooms so fair.

Verstand (Jakobus 3)

Wer von euch ist denn weise und verständig?
Wer von euch ist aktiv und bodenständig?
Er soll das durch seinen Lebenswandel zeigen,
in der Bescheidenheit, der Weisheit*s Geigen.

Wo nämlich Eifersucht und Egoismus sich verbreiten,
gibt es Unfrieden und jede Art von Gemeinheiten.
Dagegen ist die friedliche Weisheit von oben ganz rein,
Sie ist voller Erbarmen und ohne Heuchelei im Sein.

Understanding (James 3)

Which of you is wise and understanding?
Which of you is down-to-earth and acting?
Let him demonstrate this by his behaviour,
with humility, the voice behind wisdom's door.

For where jealousy and selfishness are present,
there are strife and all kinds of cruelty the end.
But the peaceful wisdom from above is pure,
full of compassion and with composure.

Streben nach Geld (Timotheus 6)

Wer unbedingt reich werden will,
um ihn herum wird oft sehr schrill
er wird sich in einem Netz von Versuchungen verfangen,
und nicht zu seinem höchsten Gut gelangen.

Er wird sich in viele unsinnige Begierden stürzen,
und nicht das Göttliche beherzen
er wird sich selbst Unheil bringen
und sie völlig zugrunde richten mit unlauteren Dingen.

Arme Seelen, reich an Geld
so mancher wird auch zum Held
und wird zu einem guten Wesen,
um zur rechten Zeit zu genesen.

Pursuit of Money (Timothy 6)

Those who desperately want to become affluent
often hold wretchedness in their hand
they will become entangled in lots of temptations
and will not attain their highest expectations.

They will plunge into many senseless desires
whoever just money admires
do not embrace the divine
and stop to value their time.

Poor souls, rich of money
not able to taste the honey
of beauty, love and honest life
towards we all should strife

Der Edle Achtfache Pfad (Buddhismus)

Rechte Ansicht
Ein Licht im Herzen, klar und rein,
Versteht des Leidens Ursprung fein.
Den Weg zu kennen, der uns führt,
Wo Schmerz vergeht, das Glück erwacht und blüht.

Rechte Absicht
Gedanken rein, von Groll befreit,
Die Seele strebt nach Klarheit, Zeit.
Entschlossen, frei von Hass und Neid,
Führt rechte Absicht zur Gelassenheit.

Rechte Sprache
Worte, die Wahrheit sanft umarmen,
Vor Lüge, Klatsch und Streit erbarmen.
Mit Herz und Weisheit klug gewählt,
Heilt Sprache, die die Welt erhält.

Rechtes Verhalten
Kein Harm, kein Schmerz durch unsre Hand,
Güte und Rücksicht – festes Band.
Im Einklang mit dem Leben gehen,
Im Wohl der andern uns verstehen.

Rechter Lebensunterhalt
Nicht andern schaden, Glück erzwingen,
Im Einklang mit dem Dasein singen.
Ein Leben wählen, das nicht quält,
Wo Mitgefühl die Welt erhält.

Rechter Einsatz

Mit Kraft und Mut, doch voller Huld,
Im Wohlwollen die Tat erfüllt.
Jeder Schritt, bedacht und rein,
Soll Menschen dienen, heiter sein.

Rechte Achtsamkeit

Der Geist, ein Fluss, der stets erwacht,
Beobachtet still die Lebensmacht.
Gedanken, Worte, Taten klar,
Im Jetzt und Hier – so wunderbar.

Rechte Konzentration

Ein stiller Fokus, sanft und weit,
Bringt Frieden in die Herzenszeit.
Auf eines ruht der Geist allein,
Und findet Ruh' im Sein, so rein.

The Noble Eightfold Path (Buddhism)

Right View
A light in the heart, so radiant, so pure,
Sees suffering's root, its truth to endure.
It knows the path where pain softly wanes,
Where joy awakens, and bliss gently reigns.

Right Intent
Pure thoughts arise, untainted by spite,
The soul seeks clarity, bathed in calm light.
Free from all hatred, from envy's cruel sting,
Right intent guides to a serene, peaceful spring.

Right Speech
Words woven gently, with truth as their guide,
Cast out all lies, let no gossip abide.
Chosen with wisdom, with heart's tender care,
They heal and uplift, sustaining the air.

Right Conduct
No harm from our hands, no pain shall we weave,
Kindness and care form the bonds we believe.
In harmony walking, with life hand in hand,
We cherish the good, in compassion we stand.

Right Livelihood
No harm to another, no force for false gain,
In tune with existence, let love's song remain.
Choose paths that bring peace, where torment's undone,
Where compassion's the root of a world gently won.

Right Commitment

With courage and grace, deeds bloom in the light,
Fulfilled with goodwill, they shine pure and bright.
Each step, calm and steady, with purpose so clear,
Serves all with serenity, drawing peace near.

Right Mindfulness

The mind, like a river, flows wakeful and free,
Observes life's soft pulse with calm clarity.
Thoughts, words, and deeds, in the present abide,
In the now's gentle wonder, where truth is our guide.

Right Concentration

A focus serene, both tranquil and vast,
Brings peace to the heart, where time's burdens are cast.
The mind rests on one, in stillness profound,
Finding rest in pure Being, where silence is found.

Inhaltsverzeichnis

www.ingramcontent.com/pod-product-compliance
Lightning Source LLC
Chambersburg PA
CBHW021132130626
46554CB00002B/968